# The Angler's Book Of British Freshwater Fish

## PAUL DUFFIELD

# CONTENTS

# THE ANGLER'S BOOK OF BRITISH FRESHWATER FISH

# 1 INTRODUCTION

This book is an reference guide for anglers to the many species of freshwater fish that can be caught the British Isles.

Colour illustrations and descriptions of all species currently listed in the official records are provided, together with information on distribution, habitat, baits and fishing methods.

The British Isles is home to many species of fish, some of which are native to these islands and some of which have been introduced either deliberately or accidentally in the recent past.

While some of these relative newcomers are welcome and have integrated into the environment, some are undesirable as they are a potential threat to native species and their habitats.

The more common undesirable species known to be present in British waters are included in the chapter on invasive species. .If you see or catch one of these species you should report it to the Environment Agency so that they can take appropriate action.

## FISH ANATOMY

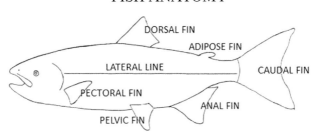

# 2 BARBEL

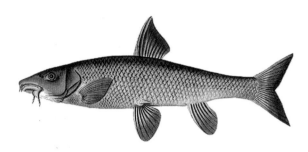

**Latin name:** Barbus barbus

**Classification:** Coarse Fish

## Current British Record

The British barbel record currently stands at 21lb 10oz (9kg 8gms) and was caught by Grahame King at Adams Mill Fishery, Bedford in 2006.

## Description

A long bodied fish with a prominent snout flanked on each side by two barbels. It is a light brown or golden colour with orange/red fins.

A distinctive fish and unlikely to be mistaken for other species. There are some general similarities with gudgeon, but gudgeon have only two barbels to the barbel's four. Close inspection, particularly of the scale pattern on the flank and the colour of the fins should confirm identification.

## Distribution

The barbel is generally a shoal fish, but some rivers contain small groups of very large specimens.

While barbel are native to the British Isles, their colonisation of some rivers systems, notably the River Severn system is relatively recent following deliberate stocking.

In the 1970's barbel became the dominant species in some parts of the River Severn, and large bags of fish around 2lb were common. Since then, the barbel has spread throughout the system, and very large specimens can be caught in the River Teme and Warwickshire Avon.

More traditional locations for large barbel are the Hampshire Avon and Dorset Stour. They are also present in other river systems such as the Thames, albeit in smaller numbers.

## Fishing Methods and Baits

While barbel can be caught on float tackle, they are usually targeted with legering tactics.

As barbel are perfectly adapted to living in very fast water, it is sometimes necessary to use very heavy weights to present a bait to them. In the faster reaches of rivers such as the River Severn, a heavy swimfeeder will get both the bait and some attractor feed to the fish.

Frequent casting is required to get a good quantity of loose feed into the swim in rivers with a strong flow. In slower swims a bed of feed such as hempseed can be introduced and a larger bait fished over the top.

A favourite bait for barbel is luncheon meat cut into cubes, but more recently pellets and boilies have become popular for the larger specimens. They can also be caught on most common coarse fishing baits such as maggots and sweetcorn.

Feeding the swim with boiled hempseed and then fishing a larger bait over the top is a popular method, the hempseed both attracting the barbel into the swim, and keeping them there.

# 3 BITTERLING

**Latin name:** Rhodeus sericeus

**Classification:** Coarse Fish (non-native)

**Current British Record**

The British bitterling record currently stands at 12dms (21gms) and was caught by D Flack from Barway Lake, Cambridgeshire in 2006.

**Description**

The bitterling has a deep body with relatively large scales and an iridescent blue stripe along the side of the body.

The bitterling could be mistaken for juvenile roach or bream, but can be identified by its larger scales.

**Distribution**

Now common in the Cheshire area and spreading east through the canal system.

**Fishing Methods and Baits**

Pole or light float tactics with small maggot baits, pellets or punched bread.

# 4 BLEAK

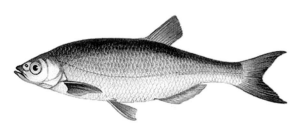

**Latin name:** Alburnus alburnus

**Classification:** Coarse Fish

**Current British Record**

The British bleak record currently stands 4oz 9dms (129gms) and was caught by D Flack from the River Lark, Cambridgeshire in 1998.

**Description**

The bleak is a small silver fish with pale coloured fins. They are a shoal fish and congregate in large numbers high up in the water, often just below the surface.

The shape of a bleak is quite similar to other British coarse fish such as dace and roach, but it is much more silver in appearance, the flank appearing to give off a silver sheen in sunlight.

**Distribution**

Bleak are primarily a river fish although they are occasionally found in some stillwaters.

A shoal fish, large numbers of them can be found near the

surface where they will often attack baits intended for other species before it has had time to fall through the water.

## Fishing Methods and Baits

Bleak are rarely the intended species of the general coarse angler, although they are sometimes targeted by match anglers as they are easy to catch and due to their large numbers can be caught in quantity to make up a match winning weight.

To catch them, use light float gear set to fish near the surface and be ready to strike as soon as you see the float or line move. Hooks should be very small, no larger than size 20 and preferably smaller.

Small maggot baits such as Pinkies or Squatts are a good bait for bleak. They can also be caught on small pellets of bread.

# 5 BREAM (COMMON / BRONZE)

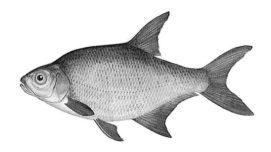

**Latin name:** Abramis brama

**Classification:** Coarse Fish

**Current British Records**

The British bronze bream record currently stands at 19lb 10z (8kg 90gms) and was caught by James Rust from a Cambridge water in 2005.

**Description**

The common bream is a deep bodied fish that is relatively thin across the body.

Common bream can grow to a large size and while small are silver in colour, large common bream can be a dark bronze colour.

The bream is a distinctive fish that is unlikely to be mistaken for other species, but many anglers confuse small common bream with the less common silver bream as when small, common bream are a silver/white colour.

Due to the wider distribution of common bream, it is likely

that most bream you catch will be common bream, but silver bream can be identified by their larger scales and larger eye compared to common bream of the same size.

## Distribution

Bream are found in stillwaters such as lakes and canals and the slower reaches of rivers.

They can grow to a very large size in gravel pits and large lakes, but specimens of several pounds can also be caught in many rivers, drains and canals.

## Fishing Methods and Baits

Bream are a shoal fish and if they can be found and encouraged to feed, very large weights are possible.

Legering for bream using a groundbait feeder is a popular method for Bream fishing but they can also be caught using long pole tactics.

On some waters known to contain large shoals of bream, anglers introduce a large quantity of cereal based groundbait prior to fishing, to encourage wandering shoals of bream to settle on the bait.

Bream have sensitive mouths, so small fine wire hooks are often used, along with very fine quivertips to indicate the least movement.

Popular baits include maggots, worms, pellets, sweetcorn and bread.

# 6 BREAM (SILVER)

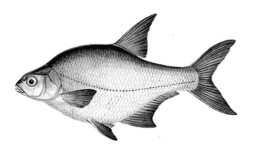

**Latin name:** Blicca bjoernika

**Classification:** Coarse Fish

**Current British Records**

The British silver bream record currently stands at 2lb 15oz (1kg 332gms) and was caught by Philip Morton from Mill Farm Fishery, Sussex in 2009.

**Description**

The silver bream is a deep bodied fish that is relatively thin across the body.

Silver bream, unlike the similar common or bronze bream, are silver as both juveniles and adults.

The silver bream is a distinctive fish that is unlikely to be mistaken for other species, but many anglers confuse small common bream with the less common silver bream as when small, common bream are a silver/white colour.

Due to the wider distribution of common bream, it is likely that most bream you catch will be common bream, but silver bream can be identified by their larger scales and larger eye compared to common bream of the same size.

## Distribution

Silver bream are found in stillwaters such as lakes and canals and the slower reaches of rivers.

## Fishing Methods and Baits

Light pole and float tactics can be used to catch silver bream. They can also be caught using maggot or groundbait swimfeeder tactics.

Popular baits include maggots, worms, pellets, sweetcorn and bread.

# 7 BULLHEAD

**Latin name:** Cottus Gobio

**Classification:** Coarse Fish

## Current British Record

The British bullhead record currently stands at 1oz (28gms) and was caught by R Johnson from Green River, near Guildford, Surrey in 1983.

## Description

Also known as the Millers Thumb, the bullhead is a small fish with a large flattened head.

Rarely targeted by anglers unless they are intent on getting into the record books with a particularly large specimen of the species, this greedy fish will often take maggots or quite large worms intended for other fish.

The bullhead is a distinctive fish that is unlikely to be mistaken for other species.

## Distribution

While not present in large numbers, bullhead can occasionally be caught in many rivers throughout the British

Isles.

## Fishing Methods and Baits

Bullhead are difficult to target specifically, but in waters where they are known to exist legering with a bunch of maggots or a worm can be successful.

# 8 CARP (COMMON)

**Latin name** Cyprinus carpio

**Classification:** Coarse Fish

## Current British Record

The British common carp record currently stands at 67lb 8oz (30kg 618gms) and was caught by Austin Holness from Conningbrook Lake, Ashford, Kent in 2008.

## Description

The common carp is a deep bodied fish with large scales, a pair of barbels and a dorsal fin with a thick base.

The fully scaled variety has large scales which vary from dark bronze to silver in colour.

Largely due to selective breeding in the past, some common carp have just a few large scales and some have very few or no scales at all. These scale variations have led to the terms 'fully scaled common', 'leather carp' and 'mirror carp' but all are of the same species.

Once regarded as almost impossible to catch, carp are now

the most widely caught fish in the British Isles, having been stocked in large numbers into commercial fisheries where they are popular with both match and pleasure anglers.

## Fishing Methods and Baits

Smaller carp can be caught by most float fishing and legering techniques, as well as floating baits such as bread crust.

Larger carp are usually fished for with specialist leger rigs, and by stalking individual fish with float fished or free lined baits.

On heavily stocked commercial fisheries, carp will take most baits including maggots, bread, worms, sweetcorn and pellets.

Boilies are a popular bait for larger specimens.

# 9 CARP (CRUCIAN)

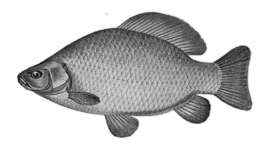

**Latin name:** Carassius carassius

**Classification:** Coarse Fish

### Current British Record

The British crucian carp record currently stands at 4lb 9oz 9dms (2kg 85gms) and was caught by M Bowler from RMC Fishery, Yately Lake in 2003.

### Description

The crucian carp is a deep bodied stocky fish, similar in appearance to the common carp, but does not grow as large. Primarily a still water fish, it is found in many pools and small lakes. Some rivers and canals also hold small populations.

A spirited fighter, easily recognisable by its rich golden colour, the crucian carp is a popular fish with anglers, and if you find a shoal of them you can have a good day's sport.

### Fishing Methods and Baits

Pole or light float tactics with maggots, bread, worms, sweetcorn and pellets.

# 10 CARP (GRASS)

**Latin name:** Ctenopharyngodon idella

**Classification:** Coarse Fish (non-native)

**Current British Record**

The British grass carp record currently stands at 44lb 8z (20kg 185gms) and was caught by Phillip Kingsbury from Horton Church Lake in 2006.

The record list for this species was closed on 31 October 2007 and no further record claims will be considered.

**Description**

The grass carp is a has a long thin body, dark tail and bronze scales. They are often mistaken for large chub, but can be identified by their smaller mouth and the position of the eye which is much lower than chub.

**Distribution**

The grass carp is not native to the British Isles and was introduced to many fisheries for weed control as they will readily eat weed and other plants.

Since their introduction they can be found in waters over much of the British Isles, but are usually only present in small numbers.

**Fishing Methods and Baits**

Float and leger tactics can be used to catch grass carp using a variety of baits including bread, sweetcorn and pellets.

# 11 CATFISH (BLACK BULLHEAD)

**Latin name:** Ameiurus melas

**Classification:** Coarse Fish (non-native)

**Current British Record**

The British black bullhead catfish record currently stands at 1lb 3oz 1dms (539gms) and was caught by K Clements from Lake Meadows, Billericay, Essex in 2001.

**Description**

The black bullhead catfish has barbels located near its mouth, a broad head, spiny fins and no scales.

It can be distinguished from the more common wels catfish by a tan crescent around its tail. It is also less streamlined in shape than the Wels catfish.

**Distribution**

The black bullhead catfish is not widely distributed in the British Isles but occasional captures are reported. Small populations are thought to exist in some waters due to escapes from ornamental and garden ponds.

## Fishing Methods and Baits

Catfish are largely nocturnal and feed during the night, but young catfish may feed during the day.

Likely to accept most baits including maggots, worms, pellets and bread.

# 12 CATFISH (WELS)

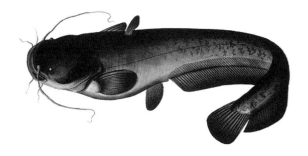

**Latin name:** Silurus glanis

**Classification:** Coarse Fish (non-native)

## Current British Record

The British wels catfish record currently stands at 62lb (28kg 123gms) and was caught by R Garner from Withy Pool, Henley, Bedfordshire in 1997.

The record list for this species was closed on 31 October 2007 and no further record claims will be considered.

## Description

The European catfish, also knows as the wels catfish is a powerful fish capable of growing to a large size.

It has a large mouth flanked by 6 barbels and a long anal fin. Colour is variable, usually with dark marbling & spots against a pale background.

Although not regarded as an invasive species, catfish may only be stocked in fully enclosed stillwaters due to the risks they pose to native fish and their habitats.

## Distribution

The catfish is found in only a few waters in the British Isles, mainly lakes where it has been stocked, but some rivers hold individual specimens.

## Fishing Methods and Baits

Baits presented either on float or leger tackle will take catfish, but the size and power of these fish dictates that the tackle must be strong.

Catfish will take most baits intended for carp and pike.

Favourite baits are dead baits, shrimp and squid. Fishmeal boilies have also been known to catch catfish.

# 13 CHARR (ARCTIC)

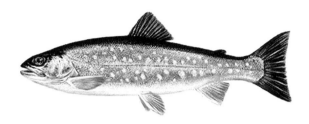

**Latin name:** Salvelinus alpinus

**Classification:** Game Fish

## Current British Record

The British arctic charr record currently stands at 9lb 8oz (4kg 309gms) and was caught by W Fairbairn from Loch Arkaig, Inverness Scotland in 1995.

## Description

The arctic charr is a coldwater fish closely related to salmon. It is mostly silver in colour, with light coloured spots. It can easily be distinguished from coarse fish by the small adipose fin, common to game fish, that is located near the tail.

## Distribution

The arctic charr is one of the rarest native fish in the British Isles. It is mostly found in Scotland, but is also present in deep mountain lakes in England and Wales such as the Lake District.

## Fishing Methods and Baits

Charr can be caught using artificial flies or spinners fished deep.

# 14 CHUB

**Latin name:** Leuciscus cephalus

**Classification:** Coarse Fish

## Current British Record

The British chub record currently stands at 9lb 5oz (4kg 224gms) and was caught by Andy Maker from a southern stillwater in 2007.

## Description

The chub has a large mouth, thick set body and dark edged scales. It lives primarily in rivers, but can also be found in some lakes and canals.

Small chub can be found in shoals while larger chub are often more solitary creatures with their own territories.

The chub is a favourite of river anglers and even very small rivers can hold quite large specimens, usually occupying the deeper pools where they make their home among the sunken roots of trees and bushes.

## Fishing Methods and Baits

A roving approach is usually best for catching chub in small and medium sized rivers. A leger rig using just enough weight to hold bottom should be cast into any likely spot near bushes or trees in the deeper parts of the river.

Sensitive bite detection is rarely necessary as chub bite boldly and it pays to keep your hand on the rod when waiting for a bite.

After you have caught one, or perhaps two chub from a swim, it is time to move on. If you have a stretch of river pretty much to yourself, you can bait several swims with mashed or liquidised bread, and then fish each in turn, hopefully taking a fish or two from each as you return along the bank.

Tread carefully and try to be inconspicuous, especially on small rivers. Although chub will take a bait boldly, they are a cautious fish, and can seem to disappear into the depths if they are disturbed by an angler moving against the skyline or causing a noisy vibration on the bank.

Chub will take almost any bait at times, including maggots and worms where there are not too many smaller fish to take the bait first, but firm favourites are bread in all its forms and cheese either used on its own or mixed with breadcrumbs to make a strongly flavoured paste.

# 15 DACE

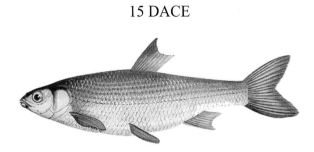

**Latin name:** Leuciscus leuciscus

**Classification:** Coarse Fish

**Current British Record**

The British dace record currently stands at 1b 5oz 2dms (599gms) and was caught by Simon Aston from the river Wear in 2002.

**Description**

Dace are slim silver fish that are very similar in appearance to small chub.

Dace do not grow very large, and one of near to 1lb would be a very good specimen. What they lack in size, they make up in numbers and large shoals of them can often be seen on or near the surface of rivers in the summer months.

The dace is widely distributed, but prefers fast flowing water so is mostly found in rivers although there are small populations of dace in some still waters.

**Fishing Methods and Baits**

Light float fishing methods on rivers will account for dace

where they will often be caught as part of a mixed bag with roach.

Being primarily 'up in the water' feeders, a lightly shotted rig that allows the bait to fall slowly through the swim will usually work best, but a light swimfeeder rig fished in conjunction with a very sensitive quivertip can work on days when the fish are feeding on the bottom.

You will need quick reactions when dace fishing as they can eject the bait very quickly and a fast strike is required.

Dace are generally fished for with using small baits such as maggots and small pieces of bread but larger specimens can be caught using bread flake, paste and worms.

# 16 EEL

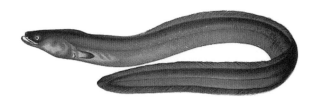

**Latin name:** Anguilla anguilla

**Classification:** Coarse Fish

### Current British Record

The British eel record currently stands at 11b 2oz (5kg 46gms) and was caught by S Terry from Kingfisher Lake, near Ringwood, Hampshire in 1978.

### Description

Although technically the eel is not a fish, it is often caught by anglers and is included in the licence for coarse fish.

The eel has declined significantly in recent years due to the effects of global warming.. It is widely distributed throughout British waters, but is most likely to be encountered in number in rivers and drains.

Eels can grow very large, the larger specimens occasionally being caught by pike anglers fishing with dead baits.

### Fishing Methods and Baits

Eels will take most live baits used by anglers such as maggots and worms and where present in large numbers they are often caught by anglers targeting other fish on both float and leger tackle.

The larger specimens mostly feed at night and will take dead baits of whole or sectioned coarse and sea fish.

# 17 GOLDFISH (BROWN)

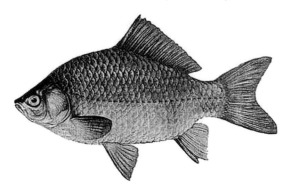

**Latin name:** Carassius auratus

**Classification:** Coarse Fish (non-native)

## Current British Record

The British brown goldfish record currently stands at 51b 11oz 8dms (2kg 594gms) and was caught by D Lewis from a Surrey stillwater in 1994.

## Description

The brown goldfish is an Asian species that has become established in the British Isles relatively recently and is present in stillwaters across England and Wales.

The natural form of the decorative goldfish kept as pets, it resembles a small carp in appearance and readily hybridises with native populations of crucian carp.

## Fishing Methods and Baits

Pole, float and leger tactics on a variety of baits including maggots, worms, bread and pellets.

# 18 GRAYLING

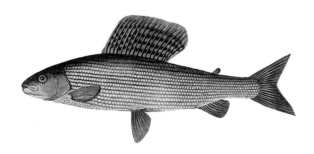

**Latin name:** Thymallus thymallus

**Classification:** Game Fish

**Current British Record**

The British grayling record currently stands at 41b 4oz 8dms (1kg 940gms) and was caught by Paul Mildred from a Wessex river in 2009.

**Description**

The grayling known as 'the lady of the stream' is a silver coloured fish with a large sail shaped dorsal fin and an additional adipose fin near the tail that is also found in game fish such as trout.

Grayling are usually be found in the faster parts of rivers.

As grayling spawn at the same time as coarse fish, they are popular with game anglers as they allow fly fishing methods to be used when trout are not in season.

**Fishing Methods and Baits**

Grayling where present in reasonable numbers can be taken

on maggots in a mixed bag of dace and roach, but are more often fished for by game anglers using artificial flies.

Float fishing with maggots is a good method for catching grayling, but they will also take legered baits.

Fly fishing is also a popular method for catching grayling and they will take both dry (floating) and wet (sinking) flies.

There are a number of fly patterns developed especially for grayling fishing, but they will also take flies intended for trout.

# 19 GUDGEON

**Latin name:** Gobio gobio

**Classification:** Coarse Fish

**Current British Record**

The British gudgeon record currently stands at 5oz (141gms) and was caught by D H Hull from the River Nadder, Sutton Mandeville, Wiltshire in 1994.

**Description**

Gudgeon are a small fish that resemble small barbel. They are present in a wide variety of waters.

Some canals have very large populations of gudgeon, but the larger specimens are to be found in rivers where they are often caught by anglers targeting other species such as roach and dace.

Gudgeon feed freely and boldly, often pulling the float several inches below the surface. They are most likely to be caught down in the water, on or near the bed of the river or canal.

**Fishing Methods and Baits**

Gudgeon can be caught using pole, float and legering

techniques. Where they are present in large numbers, fishing close in with a small whip is an effective method for catching gudgeon.

Small amounts of loose feed and groundbait should be fed regularly to keep the gudgeon in the swim and feeding.

It often pays to feed two or three different lines, and switch to another when bites slow on one line. Continue feeding all lines, and over the course of a session you can catch a large number of gudgeon.

# 20 LOACH

**Latin name:** Barbatula barbatula

**Classification:** Coarse Fish

**Current British Record**

The British loach record currently stands at 7dms (13gms) and was caught by Geoffrey Green from the Windmill Fishery in 2005.

**Description**

The loach is a small fish with barbels that rarely exceeds a few inches in length.

They are more likely to be caught by small boys with a net, than an angler with rod and line, although the odd one may be caught when legering small baits in small rivers.

**Fishing Methods and Baits**

If you are intent on catching every species of fish that swims using rod and line, you may be lucky if you persevere with a small maggot or a piece of a small red worm on light leger tackle where Loach are known to be present.

# 21 MINNOW

**Latin name:** Phoxinus phoxinus

**Classification:** Coarse Fish

### Current British Record

The British minnow record currently stands at 13.5dms (24gms) and was caught by J Sawyer from Whitworth Lake, Spennymoor in 1998.

### Description

The minnow is a very small fish with dark markings along the flank. It has quite a blunt snout and very small scales.

Minnows are found, sometimes in very large quantities, in lakes and rivers where they swim in large shoals.

Generally regarded as a nuisance fish when they snatch a bait intended for larger species, minnows are rarely fished for deliberately except by very small boys and anglers who require a quantity to use as live bait for perch or trout.

### Fishing Methods and Baits

When all else fails, a few minnows snatched using a pinkie on a light whip rig at the end of a disappointing day can be fun, especially as in clear water they are often found in large shoals very close to the bank and larger individuals can be targeted by sight.

Almost any small bait will be taken by minnows, several of them often racing to take a small maggot or piece of bread at the same time.

# 22 ORFE (GOLDEN)

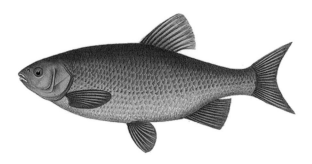

**Latin name:** Leuciscus idus

**Classification:** Coarse Fish (non-native)

## Current British Record

The British golden orfe record currently stands at 8lb 5oz (3kg 770gms) and was caught by M Wilkinson at Lymm Vale, Cheshire in 2000.

## Description

The orfe is a bright orange fish that has been introduced in many commercial fisheries. They are a slimmer fish than ornamental goldfish that they resemble from a distance.

## Distribution

While not naturally present in the British Isles, they are widely distributed throughout England and Wales in commercial fisheries.

## Fishing Methods and Baits

Pole, float and legering tactics will catch orfe and they will often take a floating bait such as bread.

# 23 PERCH

**Latin name:** Perca fluviatilis

**Classification:** Coarse Fish

**Current British Record**

The British perch record currently stands at 6lb 3oz (2kg 800gms) and was caught by Neil Stephen from Stream Valley Lakes, Crowborough, Sussex in 2010.

**Description**

The perch is a very distinctive fish with a large spiked dorsal fin and striped markings. They are bold voracious fish, and a small perch is often the first fish caught by young Anglers as they are not tackle shy and bite boldly.

Populations of perch exist in most British waters. Small perch live in shoals, whilst the largest specimens tend to be solitary.

**Fishing Methods and Baits**

Small perch can be taken on most float fishing and legering

methods where they will often make up part of a mixed bag.

Where large perch are known to be present they can be caught using small spinners.

Small perch will take maggots and worms, the larger fish being caught on small fish baits, large worms and artificial spinning baits.

Legering with large worms such as lobs and dendrobaenas is a good technique that can account for some quite sizable perch.

# 24 PIKE

**Latin name:** Esox lucius

**Classification:** Coarse Fish

**Current British Record**

The British pike record currently stands at 46lb 13oz (21kg 234gms) and was caught by R Lewis from Llandegfedd, Wales in 1992.

**Description**

The pike is a predatory fish that can grow to a very large size. It is a long fish, built for bursts of speed, and with a mouth full of sharp teeth for seizing its prey.

Well camouflaged in bands of dark and light green or black, it is able to lurk unseen among reeds and other plants from which it can emerge vary quickly to seize prey fish that pass by.

**Fishing Methods and Baits**

Small pike will take maggots and worms, but the larger specimens are caught using live and dead fish baits as well as artificial lures such as spinners, spoons, plugs and the more recent jelly baits.

Pike will generally be found where there is cover that will hide them from their prey.

A lure will often work well if pulled through the water near lily pads and reeds. Most lures are capable of catching pike and often a single fish can be targeted if sighted.

Pike will often emerge from underwater vegetation to follow a lure, and it often pays to speed up the rate of retrieve when this happens to goad the pike into taking what appears to be a prey fish trying to escape.

Live baits, where allowed, will account for pike either fished under a heavy float and allowed to swim freely, or on a paternoster float-leger rig. Most coarse fish are suitable as live bait, but the practice is not always allowed.

Where live baiting is not permitted, pike can also be taken on dead baits, including sea fish such as mackerel, sprats and herring. These can be fished either on a paternoster float rig or leger rig.

# 25 PUMPKINSEED

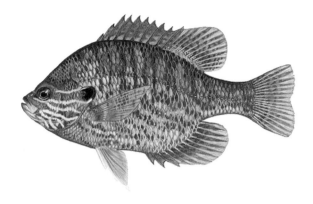

**Latin name:** Lepomis gibbosus

**Classification:** Coarse Fish (non-native)

### Current British Record

The British pumpkinseed record currently stands at 14oz 2dms (400gms) and was caught by B Rushmer from Tanyards Fishery, Sussex in 2003.

### Description

The pumpkinseed is a brightly coloured fish that is unlike any native species. It has a single dorsal fin that is divided into two parts, the first part having several spines. It also has a distinctive spot on the gill cover.

### Distribution

Although not a native species, pumpkinseed have been present in some British waters for many years. There are established populations in rivers and lakes in southern

England.

## Fishing Methods and Baits

Pumpkinseed can be caught using pole and light float tactics and will take most baits including maggots, worms and pellets.

# 26 ROACH

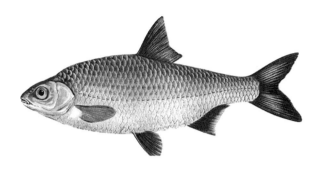

**Latin name:** Rutilus rutilus

**Classification:** Coarse Fish

**Current British Record**

The British roach record currently stands at 4lb 4oz (1kg 927gms) and was caught by Keith Berry from a Northern Ireland stillwater in 2006.

**Description**

The roach is a silver fish with red fins, present in most British coarse fishing waters.

Most coarse anglers will have caught a roach early in their fishing career as they are a free feeding shoal fish that will take most small baits.

**Fishing Methods and Baits**

Most coarse fishing tactics will catch roach depending on the type of water and conditions.

In rivers they can be fished for with light tackle by trotting a stick float with the stream, using maggots as the bait and ensuring a steady stream of free offerings are thrown in to keep the roach in the swim and competing for food.

Larger river specimens can be taken using a leger or swimfeeder rig, with larger baits such as worm, bread flake or paste allowing selective targeting of the larger specimens.

In ponds, lakes and canals, pole or whip tactics can account for large bags of small or medium sized roach using pinkies or maggots with a cloud groundbait.

# 27 RUDD

**Latin name:** Scardinius erythrophthalmus

**Classification:** Coarse Fish

## Current British Record

The British rudd record currently stands at 4lb 10oz (2kg 97gms) and was caught by Simon Parry from a Freshwater Lake, County Armagh, Northern Ireland in 2001.

## Description

The rudd is a similar fish to the roach, but is often a more golden colour and slightly deeper in the body. While less common than the roach, the rudd is widely distributed throughout British stillwater coarse fisheries such as ponds, lakes and canals as well as slow moving rivers.

In waters where roach and rudd exist together they will often be taken in a mixed bag, the rudd often feeding higher in the water than roach and taking baits on or near the surface.

## Fishing Methods and Baits

In ponds, lakes and canals, pole or whip tactics can account for large bags of small or medium sized Rudd using pinkies or maggots with a cloud groundbait.

In addition to float and leger tactics, rudd can be taken by presenting floating bread flake and this is a popular method for targeting the larger specimens.

Rudd will also take an artificial fly presented with fly tackle.

# 28 RUFFE

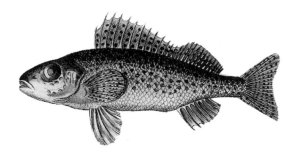

**Latin name:** Gymnocephalus cernuus

**Classification:** Coarse Fish

## Current British Record

The British ruffe record currently stands at 5oz 4dms (148gms) and was caught by R J Jenkins from West View Farm, Cumbria in 1986.

## Description

The ruffe is similar in appearance to the perch, but with a drab colouring in comparison to the bold stripes of the perch.

Ruffe do not grow to a large size, and although they are quite widespread they do not exist in large numbers and are not regularly encountered by most Anglers.

## Fishing Methods and Baits

Ruffe are not usually deliberately targeted by Anglers but where they are present they can be taken by most float fishing and legering methods on maggot and worm.

# 29 SALMON (ATLANTIC)

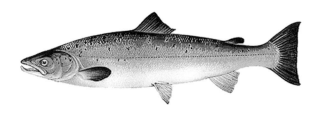

**Latin name:** Salmo Salar

**Classification:** Game Fish

**Current British Record**

The British Atlantic salmon record currently stands at 64lb (29kg 29gms) and was caught by Miss G W Ballatine from the River Tay, Scotland in 1922.

## Description

The Atlantic salmon has a long, thin silver body, a large mouth and the small adipose fin common to game fish just in front of the tail. It also has dark spots on the head and the body above the lateral line.

There are similarities between the Atlantic salmon and the sea trout, however, the salmon has a more streamlined shape, a concave tail and slimmer tail wrist. It also has few or no spots below the lateral line and the upper jaw does not extend beyond the rear of the eye.

## Distribution

The Atlantic salmon is a migratory fish that can be caught in many rivers in the British Isles.

**Fishing Methods and Baits**

Atlantic salmon are caught using a variety of methods and baits including artificial spinner, artificial fly, worm and prawn.

# SALMON PARR

The salmon parr is the juvenile form of the salmon and is often caught by anglers fishing for trout.

It can be distinguished from young trout by a more streamlined body shape, deep forked tail and longer pectoral fin. It also has less spots on the gill cover, typically less than four and often only one.

# 30 SALMON (PACIFIC HUMPED BACK)

**Latin name:** Oncorhynchus gorbuscha

**Classification:** Game Fish

### Current British Record

The British pacific humped back salmon record currently stands at 3lb 8oz 12dms (1kg 609gms) and was caught by Louis Hunter from the River Tweed, Scotland in 2007.

### Description

The pacific humped back salmon is a distinctive fish having a humped back, large oval-shaped black spots above the lateral line, a v-shaped tail and a small adipose fin, common to game fish, just before the tail.

### Distribution

This species is not native to the British Isles, but a small number of captures have been reported in recent years.

### Fishing Methods and Baits

Likely to take the same baits as Atlantic salmon including artificial spinner, artificial fly, worm and prawn.

# 31 SCHELLY (SKELLY)

**Latin name:** Coregonus Lavaretus

**Classification:** Coarse Fish

## Current British Record

The British schelly record currently stands at 2lb 1oz 9dms (950gms) and was caught by S M Barrie from Haweswater Reservoir, Cumbria in 1986.

## Description

The schelly is a silver coloured fish with a forked tail. Although it has a small adipose fin just before the tail which is present in game fish it is It is designated as a coarse fish.

## Distribution

The schelly is only found in the Lake District in Cumbria.

## Fishing Methods and Baits

The schelly is in decline and is now a protected species. Fishing for this species is no longer allowed.

# 32 STICKLEBACK

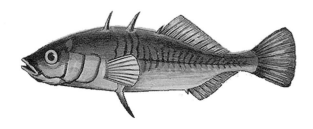

**Latin name:**
Gasterosteus aculeatus (3 spined stickleback)
Pungitius pungitius (10 Spined Stickleback)

**Classification:** Coarse Fish

**Current British Record**

The British 3 spined stickleback record currently stands at 4dms (7gms) and was caught by D Flack, High Flyer Lake, Ely, Cambridgeshire in 1998.

**Description**

Easily recognisable, and possibly the best known British freshwater fish, these fish have three or ten spines along the back before the dorsal fin.

Of the two, the three spined stickleback is the most common and is found everywhere from small ditches to rivers and lakes. The ten spined stickleback is more rare, and is found in stagnant waters in mud and weed.

**Fishing Methods and Baits**

Whilst not a fish you would deliberately target, you may get one when using a small maggot or worm as bait.

If a worm is only hooked once in the middle of the body, you may even get two at once, one on each end as they are not often hooked, but can suck in quite a large length of a thin red worm or brandling and will remain attached after you lift your tackle out of the water.

# 33 TENCH

**Latin name:** Tinca tinca

**Classification:** Coarse Fish

## Current British Record

The British tench record currently stands at 15lb 3oz 6dms (6kg 888gms) and was caught by D Ward from an undisclosed stillwater in 2001.

## Description

The tench is a thick set fish with a distinctive olive green or brown colouring. A large tail fin is a feature of this species which allows it to swim strongly. Tench will often be found in the margin areas among lily pads and thick weed.

A popular fish with anglers primarily in the summer months, tench are widespread throughout British waters, but most likely to be encountered in lakes, ponds, slow flowing rivers and some canals.

## Fishing Methods and Baits

Tench are bottom feeding fish, so float tackle set to present the bait on the bottom is a popular and successful method.

Tench bites are rarely bold or fast and knowing when to strike can be difficult for inexperienced anglers. Sometimes it is necessary to wait for a positive indication, on other days an earlier strike is needed.

Tench can also be caught using leger tactics, and are often caught by anglers targeting carp.

Most baits will take tench, popular baits being maggots, worms, sweetcorn, bread and small boilies.

# 34 TROUT (AMERICAN BROOK/BROOK CHAR)

**Latin name:** Salvelinus fontinalis

**Classification:** Game Fish (non-native)

## Current British Record

The British American brook trout record currently stands at 8lb 3oz (9kg 8gms) and was caught by E Holland from Fontburn Reservoir, Northumberland in 1998.

## Description

The American brook trout is a green or brown colour with a distinctive marbled pattern of lighter shades and red spots along the flank and back. In common with other game fish it has a small adipose fin just before the tail.

## Distribution

The American brook trout is not native to the British Isles, but has been stocked into British waters on occasion, notably in the 1970s and 1980s.

They are not widely distributed in the British Isles as most stockings have not been successful, but naturalised populations are believed to exist in some areas.

## Fishing Methods and Baits

Where they are present it is likely that the only permitted method will be fly fishing. American brook trout prefer deep water, so where naturalised populations exist, wet fly fished deep is probably the most successful method.

# 35 TROUT (BROWN)

**Latin name:** Salmo trutta

**Classification:** Game Fish

**Current British Record**

The British natural brown trout record currently stands at 31lb 12oz (14kg 401gms) and was caught by Brian Rutland from Lock Awe, Argull, Scotland in 2002.

The British cultivated brown trout record currently stands at 28lb 1oz (12kg 729gms) and was caught by D Taylor from Dever Springs Trout Fishery, Hants in 1995.

**Description**

The brown trout is the only species of trout that is native to the British Isles.

There are wide colour variations in populations in different parts of the country from silver to brown or gold with a variable number of spots.

In common with other game fish the brown trout has a small adipose fin just before the tail.

## Distribution

The brown trout is widely distributed throughout the British Isles. It is the predominant species in many small rivers and streams and smaller numbers are also present in many rivers that also contain coarse fish.

In addition to these native populations, many commercial trout fisheries stock cultivated brown trout.

## Fishing Methods and Baits

On waters where native brown trout are the predominant species and on most commercial trout fisheries, only fishing with artificial fly is allowed.

Spinning for natural brown trout is allowed in some lakes and reservoirs, and where they exist alongside coarse fish, brown trout will also take maggots and worms.

# 36 TROUT (RAINBOW)

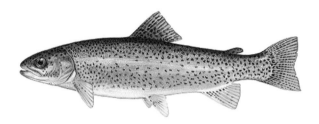

**Latin name:** Oncorhynchus mykiss

**Classification:** Game Fish (non-native)

## Current British Record

The British cultivated rainbow trout record currently stands at 33lb 4oz 15dms (15kg 82gms) and was caught by J Lawson from Watercress Trout Fishery in 2003.

The British resident rainbow trout record (a fish previously stocked that has been resident in it's location for many years) currently stands at 24lb 1oz 4dms (10kg 921gms) and was caught by J Hammond from Hanningfield Reservoir, Essex in 1998.

## Description

The rainbow trout resembles the native brown trout but has a distinctive rainbow colouring along its flank and smaller spots.

In common with other game fish the rainbow trout has a small adipose fin just before the tail.

## Distribution

Many commercial trout fisheries stock cultivated rainbow trout and they are also stocked in many man made reservoirs.

## Fishing Methods and Baits

Fishing is with artificial fly only in most fisheries, but where allowed, rainbow trout may also be caught using spinners. If fishing with live baits is permitted they will also take maggots and worms.

# 37 TROUT (SEA)

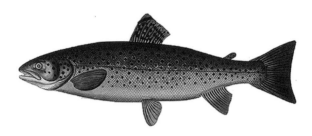

**Latin name:** Salmo trutta

**Classification:** Game Fish

### Current British Record

The British sea trout record currently stands at 28lb 5oz 4dms (12kg 850gms) and was caught by J Farrent from Calshot Spit, River Test in 1992.

### Description

The sea trout is the same species as brown trout. After spending time at sea, it returns to the river to spawn. It has a long, thin silver body, a large mouth and the small adipose fin common to game fish just in front of the tail. It also has dark spots on the head and the body.

There are similarities between the Atlantic salmon and the sea trout, however, the salmon has a more streamlined shape, a concave tail and slimmer tail wrist. It also has few or no spots below the lateral line and the upper jaw does not extend beyond the rear of the eye.

### Fishing Methods and Baits

Sea trout are usually fished for at night using artificial flies.

# 38 WALLEYE

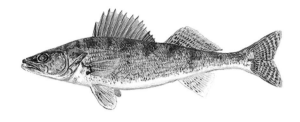

**Latin name:** Stizostedion vitreum

**Classification:** Coarse Fish (non-native)

### Current British Record

The British walleye record currently stands at 11lb 12oz (5kg 329gms) and was caught by F Adams from the River Delph, Welney, Norfolk in 1934.

The record list for this species was closed on 31 October 2007 and no further record claims will be considered.

### Description

The walleye is a predatory fish that looks like an elongated perch. . It is sometimes referred to as a pike-perch due to its similarities with both fish but it is a separate species.

It is olive and gold in colour with dark bands along its back.

### Distribution

Although a small number were stocked in the early 20th century it is believed that these have now died out and that the species is no longer present in the British Isles.

# 39 ZANDER

**Latin name:** Stizostedion lucioperca

**Classification:** Coarse Fish (non-native)

### Current British Record

The British zander record currently stands at 21lb 5oz (9kg 667gms) and was caught by James Benfield from the River Severn at Upper Load Lock in 2007.

### Description

The zander is a powerful predator that can grow to a large size. It is sometimes referred to as a pike-perch due to its similarities with both fish but it is a separate species.

Whilst not as widely distributed as either the pike or the perch, large populations exist in some rivers and canals.

### Fishing Methods and Baits

Zander are generally fished for using live and dead fish baits as well as artificial lures such as spinners, spoons, plugs and the more recent jelly baits.

Live baits, where allowed, will account for zander either

fished under a heavy float and allowed to swim freely, or on a paternoster float-leger rig. Most coarse fish are suitable as live bait, but the practice is not always allowed.

Where live baiting is not permitted, zander can also be taken on dead baits, including sea fish such as mackerel, sprats and herring. These can be fished either on a paternoster float rig or leger rig.

# 40 INVASIVE SPECIES

The following non-native species are known to be present in some British waters.

If you see or catch one of these species you should report it to the Environment Agency so they can take appropriate action to protect native fish stocks.

The Environment Agency can be contacted through their website at http://www.environment-agency.gov.uk.

## STERLET AND STURGEON

**Latin name:** Acipenser spp.

### Description

A very distinctive appearance with a pointed nose and plates ('scutes') along the back and sides of the body.

### Distribution

Known to exist in some fisheries, however stocking them in stillwaters is illegal and requires an ILFA licence.

# SUNBLEAK

**Latin name:** Leucaspius delineatus

## Description

Sunbleak, also known as motherless minnows have a small slender body, similar to bleak.

They are silver in appearance with an olive green back. Other identifying features are an upturned mouth and relatively large eyes.

## Distribution

Found throughout Somerset, Hampshire and also in Dorset.

# TOPMOUTH GUDGEON

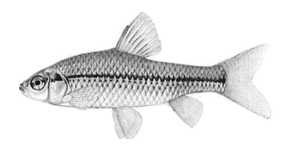

**Latin name:** Pseudorasbora parva

## Description

Distinct in appearance with rounded fins and an upturned lower jaw with a hard edge. Unlike the native gudgeon, topmouth gudgeon have no barbels.

## Distribution

isolated populations are present across England and Wales.

# 41 HYBRIDS

Many British coarse fish are capable of hybridisation. This is where the eggs of one species are fertilised by the milt of another species.

You may catch fish which closely resemble a native species, but do not look 'quite right'. Often the body shape does not conform to the natural shape of the species, or it may have fins that are the wrong shape or colour. This is the result of hybridisation, the fish being strictly neither one species or the other.

It is common for hybrids to very closely resemble on of the species more than the other. When one of the species is capable of growing to a larger size than the other, such as with bream and roach, the fish may initially appear to be a large specimen of the smaller growing species.

Common hybrids include roach/rudd, roach/bream, rudd/bream, crucian carp/common carp, crucian carp/brown goldfish.

# ACKNOWLEDGMENTS

Pictures of fish used in this book are public domain images reproduced from illustrations in 'A History of the Fishes of the British Islands' by Jonathan Couch, first published in 1862, 'Allgemeine Naturgeschichte der Fische' by Marcus Bloch, first published in 1782 and images released into the public domain by the U.S. Fish and Wildlife Service.

# ABOUT THE AUTHOR

Paul Duffield describes himself as a 'traditional angler'. Having been born early in the second half of the 20th century and fished for over 40 years, he is attempting to rediscover and recapture the magic and excitement that he experienced when he first began fishing at 10 years old.

A vintage fishing tackle enthusiast and restorer, Paul fishes with cane rods, centrepin reels and quill floats and prefers to spend a few hours on a wild stream to modern stocked stillwaters.

17546987R00047

Printed in Poland
by Amazon Fulfillment
Poland Sp. z o.o., Wrocław